Surviving
YOUR
WILDERNESS

DANIEL KOLENDA

Daniel Kolenda
with Bob Gladstone
Wilderness Survival Guide
English

Copyright © Christ for all Nations
ISBN 978-1933446-22-6

Edition 1, Printing 1
20,000 copies

Cover Design: Jaclyn Cavalier
Carlos Flores
Typesetting: Lisa Simpson

Published by: **Christ for all Nations** - CfaN.org
PO Box 590588 • Orlando, FL 32859-9927 • USA

Printed in the USA

INDEX

Surviving Your Wilderness

Introduction

"If you're going through hell, keep going!" So said Winston Churchill during one of the worst crises in world history. And these words of wisdom still apply to anyone passing through a trial today. Adversity does not have to become our destination. It can be a pathway to something greater.

Maybe you are passing through a difficult season in your life. Perhaps you feel spiritually dry and alone. You might feel as though your prayers are not being heard and you wonder if God even knows where you are. You are not alone. Millions of believers have passed through these troubled waters and experienced the same emotions. King David sang about the "deep sunless valley of the shadow of death." John of the Cross wrote of the "dark night of the soul." Even Jesus went through times of suffering when He had to offer "prayers and supplications with loud crying and tears to the One able to save Him from death" (Heb. 5:7 NASB). People often refer to such seasons as, *The Wilderness*.

The wilderness is a hard place. But it's as crucial for our lives as it is painful. While a desert season feels terribly wrong, and loneliness and despair may seem to reign, God is with you and He desires to use the wilderness for your eternal good. To reap its benefits, however, you must understand its nature and purpose. That's the reason for this book. It will look to the Bible as a spiritual "Survival Guide" for the desert – *the* supreme source of wisdom both for enduring the wilderness, as well as navigating safely through it to God's promised destination.

But first things first. If you have not been born again into the family of God, then the wisdom that follows cannot apply to you. Before a person receives the mercy of God through faith in Jesus Christ, he or she is lost in a perpetual wilderness that stretches beyond this world and into the next. And there's no way out – except one: *repent and believe the gospel.* Entering God's Kingdom by making Jesus your Lord and Savior makes you a child of the most loving, powerful, and wonderful Father. He knows how to guide and take care of you as you traverse life's journey, even when it leads you into a wilderness. His wisdom for the wilderness is what I want to explore in this book.

To do that I will adopt six tips survival experts give for those stranded in the wilderness. As you will see, the secrets for surviving a physical wilderness bear striking parallel to those for surviving a spiritual one.

Survival Tip #1

Don't Panic

Surviving a physical wilderness takes more than the skills to build a shelter, start a fire, and purify water. It requires a certain psychology, a mind-set, a *will to live* that overcomes the fear and stress associated with crisis. In fact, some people who possessed the skill still died when stranded in a physical wilderness because they lacked the will. And others who lacked the skill but had the will, found a way to survive.

Upon entering a spiritual wilderness, our tendency is often to let our imagination run wild. "Will I ever make it out?" "Why is this happening to me?" "I don't feel ready for this." "Does God not realize what I'm going through?" "Is He angry with me?" "Is He judging me?" "Is He even real?" Though it's natural to ask questions like these, obsessing over them depletes our resolve to believe God. And since these questions relate to the very nature of God, their responses must be biblically sound. That's why our study begins here. In the wilderness, perspective is everything.

So if you find yourself in a wilderness: don't panic. Take a deep breath. Take a moment to remind yourself who God is, who you are in Christ, and what the Bible says about His faithfulness during troubled times. Fear makes you susceptible to lies from the enemy. He will lie about God's faithfulness and love for you. He'll even lie about God's existence, or about how valuable you are to Him. Such lies are meant to sap you of spiritual stamina. But that's just when the "will to live" must rise – the will to live *in the Spirit* while you pass through desert regions.

For God's children in the wilderness, the "will to live" does not merely refer to a desire to survive. It refers rather to *an earnest determination to believe God.* During spiritual drought, you must determine – sometimes against all circumstances, emotions, and even the advice of friends – that God is *real.* He is good. He is faithful, and you *will* make it through to the other side with Him. Don't let the enemy or circumstances define who God is for you. Refuse to allow yourself to believe anything but God's Word. Resolve as David did during a spiritual desert: "My heart is steadfast, O God, my heart is steadfast!" (Psa. 57:7).

One of the most important things you can understand is that even when it seems like everything around you is spinning out of control, if you are a child of God, there is nothing that touches your life that is not ultimately under God's supervision. Everything in your life is somehow "Father-filtered." He loves you dearly and deeply. He is watching over you, and won't allow anything to separate you from Him.

"For I am convinced that neither death nor life, neither angels nor demons, neither the present nor the future, nor any powers, neither height nor depth, nor anything else in all creation, will be able to separate us from the love of God that is in Christ Jesus our Lord" (Rom. 8:38-39 NIV).

Allow God's invincible love to cast out all of your fear.

"Not only so, but we also glory in our sufferings, because we know that suffering produces perseverance; perseverance, character; and character, hope. And hope does not put us to shame, because God's love has been poured out into our hearts through the Holy Spirit, who has been given to us" (Rom. 5:3-5 NIV).

Survival Tip #2

Assess Your Situation

Those stranded in the wilderness must constantly evaluate their situation. They need to take stock of their resources and understand their surroundings. That way they can move forward with a level head and a good idea of what's necessary to get through.

What Are Your Resources?

If we were lost in the wilderness, our odds of survival would drastically improve if we possessed a few basic supplies like food, water, a knife, or matches. Never are these provisions more important than when our survival is at stake. This is also true for the spiritual wilderness. The resources God has given us for spiritual life are always precious, but in the wilderness we must rediscover them and cling to them like never before.

These resources are the Word of God, the fellowship of saints, and the comfort of the Holy Spirit.

The Word of God

God's Word is an oasis of truth in any spiritual desert. No matter how barren the season, it is an ever-present source of renewal and strength. It does not depend on outward circumstances to be effective. Let Christ's Word "dwell in you richly" (Col. 3:16) because "the word is near you, in your mouth and in your heart" (Rom. 10:8). When outward conditions contradict the truth, the truth must determine our *inward* condition. "You desire truth in the innermost being" (Psa. 51:6 NASB). This allows us to live and speak from our heart – the hidden chamber that stores God's Word – and not from our circumstances. "Your word I have hidden in my heart, that I might not sin against You" (Psa. 119:11).

This is especially important when the enemy takes advantage of our wilderness by flooding us with lies and temptations. Our only weapon against him is the truth of God's Word. *That* is our wisdom for the wilderness. Jesus exemplified this in His own wilderness when He responded to the devil's temptations *by quoting Scripture* (Matt. 4:1-11). He reached into His internal arsenal, found just the right texts, and fired truth back at his enemy. God's written Word has incredible power when we believe. It is our greatest resource during dry seasons.

Not only does it protect us from lies, but God's Word also reminds us of His purpose for the wilderness itself. The wilderness can knock us off kilter and make us feel like something is terribly wrong. But the truth of God's Word provides wisdom to put everything in perspective.

The two disciples walking the road to Emmaus were suffering the pain of a sudden spiritual desert. They were totally disoriented, darkened with the despondence of dashed hopes and a chilling sense of prevailing evil. Their hero had died. Jesus of Nazareth, the mighty prophet whom they thought would redeem Israel, seemed to perish in shame like a false Messiah. Religious leaders mocked and murdered Him. Now their aspirations of freedom and glory lay buried with Him. How could this have happened? How could such hope be turned so suddenly into a wasteland?

Jesus comes along incognito. He walks beside them and interviews them. He learns what they are discussing and why they are so sad. Then He completely transforms their perspective *by explaining the Scriptures to them* (Luke 24:27). "Did not the Christ have to suffer these things and then enter his glory?" (Luke 24:26 NIV). Notice that Jesus does not first reveal Himself to them in person, showing them that He is alive and well and walking right next to them. Rather, His identity remains hidden while He *explains from the written Word* that their circumstances are not dismal after all. They are necessary to God's plan of salvation. Jesus does not change their circumstances; *He changes their perspective through the wisdom of the Scriptures.* Now they will understand, not just that Jesus came back from the dead, but that the whole "tragedy" was actually God's plan from the beginning. There was no other way to forgive their sins and exalt the King. Truth from the Scriptures transformed their viewpoint, not their situation.

That is the power of God's Word. It is a most wonderful treasure when you find yourself in the desert. As you assess your resources, rediscover the Word – because in the wilderness, perspective is everything.

The Fellowship of the Saints

The wilderness does not have to be a lonely place for a child of God. It's an expedition God means for us to travel in partnership with one another. Israel experienced Egypt, the Red Sea, and the Sinai deserts *together* as a very large family. "For I do not want you to be ignorant of the fact, brothers and sisters, that our ancestors were *all* under the cloud and that they *all* passed through the sea…[into] the wilderness" (1 Cor. 10:1,5 TNIV). It's the same for us today.

God did not intend that the members of Christ's body suffer hardship alone. We belong to one another, and must feel one another's joys and pains. That is the nature of a body. "If one member suffers, all the members suffer with it; or if one member is honored, all the members rejoice with it" (1 Cor. 12:26). So during seasons of adversity, when pressure is unusually thick, emotions thin, and relief scarce, we need the strength of our spiritual family to help carry the weight of the burden. "Bear one another's burdens, and thereby fulfill the law of Christ" (Gal. 6:2 NASB).

During his congregation's spiritual wilderness, the author of Hebrews said, "Encourage one another day after day, as long as it is still called Today, so that none of you will be hardened by the deceitfulness of sin" (Heb. 3:13 NASB). Once isolated in a spiritual desert, we become especially vulnerable to discouragement and deception.

Have you ever watched a wildlife documentary where lions are hunting, on the Serengeti for instance? You will often see how a lion waits for one of the poor

17

creatures on the fringes to separate itself from the herd. The lion will single out the one who strays away from the group because the lion knows that there is safety in numbers – and the devil knows this too. The Bible says that the devil prowls around like a roaring lion looking for someone to devour. Those who isolate themselves become an easy meal for Satan. In times of pain and hardship, without the support of the body, he knows that we can easily fall prey to his temptations and traps.

One day as I was reading about the "armor of God" in Ephesians 6, I had a revelation. The passage tells us that God has provided armor for the head, the feet, the chest, and the waist; and He has also given us a shield and a sword. But then I saw something I had never noticed before – all the protection is facing forward – *there is no armor protecting the back!* At first I found this very peculiar and then suddenly verse 18 *KJV* jumped out at me, *"Praying always with all prayer and supplication in the Spirit, and watching thereunto with all perseverance for all saints."* This verse, which is mentioned in the context of the armor of God, says that we are supposed to be looking out for one another and defending each other in the battle. There is no back armor because *we* are supposed to have each others' backs. If God equipped us in such a way that we need others to watch our backs, then it is clear that He never

18

intended that we go into battle alone. God created us to need one another. This is why if you are going through a trial, a battle, or a barren season, you need to surround yourself with brothers and sisters who will pray for you and watch out for you with purpose and perseverance.

So when evaluating your resources, consider your spiritual family. Take stock of your closest comrades and harness the power of their presence and voice. Even the experts of physical survival emphasize this point. They encourage an appraisal of your team's gifts so everyone can contribute effectively to everyone else's survival. When we find ourselves in spiritual survival mode, we must do the same.

The Comfort of the Holy Spirit

Who is a more faithful comrade in the wilderness than the Holy Spirit? Whose friendship is more valuable during troubled times than the most wonderful, kind, loyal, and awesome confidante in the universe? When taking stock of your resources, remember this most precious, personal gift of His presence and fellowship. The living God, in the Person of the Holy Spirit, is going before you, walking beside you, guarding behind you, resting upon you, and dwelling within you. What more do you need?

The greater our revelation of the Holy Spirit's presence, the greater our comfort. And the greater our comfort, the less the wilderness feels like a wilderness. This is not to say that the Holy Spirit will inoculate us from all pain and suffering. Instead, it means the depth of the Holy Spirit's comfort enables us, not only to *maintain* our joy and character in the wilderness, but also to *flourish* there in Christ more than ever.

"The wilderness and the dry land shall be glad; the desert shall rejoice and blossom like the crocus; it shall blossom abundantly and rejoice with joy and singing... Then the eyes of the blind shall be opened, and the ears of the deaf unstopped; then shall the lame man leap like a deer, and the tongue of the mute sing for joy. For waters break forth in the wilderness, and streams in the desert; the burning sand shall become a pool, and the thirsty ground springs of water; in the haunt of jackals, where they lie down, the grass shall become reeds and rushes" (Isa. 35:1-2, 5-7 ESV).

How can we have a "wilderness" so colorful, alive, and exhilarating? Through the comforting, transforming presence of the Holy Spirit. This is what makes the wilderness totally worth the trouble. It gives us the opportunity to experience the Holy Spirit's comfort on a level we would never have experienced otherwise. Nothing is more valuable than the awareness of the ever-present God. If you have entered a wilderness, determine you will use this as an occasion to discover more about the magnificent reality of the Holy Spirit.

The young patriarch, Joseph, faced many difficulties as God trained him for royalty, including his unjust imprisonment in Egypt before his rise to power. At that precise part of the story, however, the narrator makes a comment that is striking for its simplicity and magnitude. "But the Lord was with Joseph" (Gen. 39:21 NASB).

21

The story already mentioned God's presence with Joseph several times. That's what made him successful in Potiphar's house. Yet now that Joseph's situation changed from his master's house to the jailhouse, his spiritual position remained the same. Just as God was before, so is He now "with Joseph" even in prison. The radical change of circumstances did not mean that God had left Joseph. He was still with His chosen vessel, directing Joseph's steps and forging his character.

But here's the secret. The Lord was not "with" Joseph merely in the physical sense while remaining detached emotionally. No, the Lord was *with* Joseph in the fullest sense of the word. He was experiencing the trial and suffering right along with His faithful servant.

The Holy Spirit enclosed Himself within Joseph's sufferings so they could go through the wilderness together, companions in the emotions and pressures of the experience.

This is how "the Spirit also helps in our weaknesses" (Rom. 8:26). He is "groaning" with us when we "groan within ourselves" (Rom. 8:26,23). His presence is not shallow and technical, but deep and intimate. The Spirit experiences our wilderness from inside us, embedded in our unique personality and perspective. Thus we can immerse ourselves in Him as He is within us. He is the One who assisted Jesus through the wilderness. He knows how to suffer the desert while fully understanding God's will and how we should pray. He knows our thoughts, weaknesses, strengths, and ways of responding to pressure. Thus He knows exactly how to help us. He is our divine strength and knows how to walk us through.

So when you assess your resources, take stock of the comforting presence of the Holy Spirit. Realize that God Himself is with you, making His fullness available to you. You are not alone. Let the Spirit's peace and strength become yours. Let His comfort comfort you, even when there is no earthly source of consolation. Then your desert will become a sanctuary, your wilderness the garden of God.

Understand Your Surroundings

Not all "wilderness" experiences are the same. Some are caused by sin or disobedience, and some are Holy Spirit training exercises. We must know what kind of "wilderness" we are in so we can know how to respond. Let's take a look at each one.

The Wilderness of Opposition

Sin can reroute us into a spiritual wasteland. When the Israelites rebelled against the Lord, He multiplied their years in the desert. "You will suffer for your sins and know what it is like to have me against you," He told them (Num. 14:34 NIV 1984). Most of Israel's wilderness was a "wilderness of opposition" – God's opposition to their disobedience and unbelief (Heb. 3:17-19).

Sin is an evil power that stands contrary to God. When we allow unresolved sin to grow and become habit, not only do we experience a wilderness of separation, but also of divine *resistance*. "You adulterous people, don't you know that friendship with the world means enmity against God? ...That is why Scripture says: God *opposes* the proud…" (James 4:4,6 NIV).

Trying to walk against the stiff headwind of God's resistance is an unnecessary and exhausting and futile

23

activity. It is the wilderness of opposition. How then do we escape? James continues,

"But He... gives grace to the humble. Submit therefore to God. Resist the devil and he will flee from you. Draw near to God and He will draw near to you. Cleanse your hands, you sinners; and purify your hearts, you double-minded. Be miserable and mourn and weep; let your laughter be turned into mourning and your joy to gloom. Humble yourselves in the presence of the Lord, and He will exalt you" (James 4:6-10 NASB). In other words, James is saying, "Repent." Forsake your sin and turn fully to God.

Contrary to popular opinion, "repentance" is not a bad word. It is not the voice of spiritual tyranny or the rant of an angry street preacher waving his Bible – and spewing insults – at passersby. Repentance is not legalism. It is not the demand of controlling leaders, bad religion, or an irate God.

The call to repentance is God's merciful invitation to receive forgiveness, change our ways, become healed, and escape sin's power. It is God's extravagantly kind insistence that our sins do not have the last word; we are not doomed to remain in our bad habits. Repentance paves the only roadway out of the wilderness of opposition.

But we must understand what repentance is. What James describes is not just a change of behavior – even a radical change of behavior. Repentance is a total reshaping of mind and lifestyle *that centers on Jesus Christ*. Genuine repentance is not as much a matter of turning *from* sin as turning *to* Jesus. "Turn to Me and be saved, all the ends of the earth; for I am God, and there is no other" (Isa. 45:22 NASB).

If my destination is north, but I am traveling northeast, it does not help to make a complete U-turn. Making a U-turn is a radical response to finding out I was headed in the wrong direction, but it does not send me in the right direction. It sends me southwest, not north. Change according to my own wisdom is not enough, however radical my new direction may seem to be.

If repentance were always about making 180-degree U-turns, then it would only be for people who live in the most flagrant, vicious sins, moving in a direction precisely opposite to Christ. Such repentance would have no relevance for those who walk with the Lord, aim to please Him, but get slightly off course. But when we realize that repentance is less about turning *from* sin than turning *to* Jesus, we learn that repentance is something that we can do anytime the Spirit convicts us even of the subtlest sin. So if we're only a couple degrees off – maybe an attitude or mind-set gets out of sync with the Spirit – we can recalibrate so that we're once again aligned with Christ.

This is a very important principle. Many have prolonged their wilderness by focusing on the wrong thing. They've been dwelling on their failures and shortcomings. They beat themselves up, living under a constant barrage of condemnation and shame. "I will never overcome this issue. I'll never be able to live like a true Christian...." Time and time again they try to turn away from their sins, but with no victory. The sense of guilt, shame, and unworthiness has even caused some to turn away from Christ. Thus they extend their wilderness indefinitely – a far worse situation than their original struggle.

But when we turn from sin to Jesus Christ everything changes. *Jesus* is the beauty of holiness (Rev. 1:12-20). *Jesus* is our magnificent obsession (Phil. 3:7-11). *Jesus* is the baptizer in the Holy Spirit (Matt. 3:11), who empowers us to live victoriously (Rom. 8:13). *Jesus* is the great High Priest who sympathizes with our weaknesses and helps us when we're tempted (Heb. 4:14-16). *Jesus* is our life (Col. 3:1-4). Rather than thinking about how much we've failed, let's focus on Jesus Himself. That's what repentance is. If you find yourself in a wilderness caused by sin, rebellion, or disobedience, put your eyes back on Jesus and turn to Him with your whole heart. Move in the direction of Christ and you will find your way out of the wilderness of opposition.

The Wilderness of Promotion

Israel's "wilderness of opposition" actually began as a "wilderness of promotion." Their disobedience delayed their promotion for forty years. God's original plan, however, was to train Israel in the desert only for a short time – no more than two years. But why would God train His people in a desert?

God promised His people that He would "bring them up from [Egypt] to a good and large land, to a land flowing with milk and honey" (Exod. 3:8). This land would be their home forever (Isa. 60:21); the "glory of all lands" (Ezek. 20:6); the place from which Israel would keep the Lord's commandments (Psa. 105:44-45), and radiate His greatness to the other nations (Isa. 42:6). In their land, Israel would flourish as heaven's Kingdom on earth, a supernatural light embodying the glory of God's character to the world.

That is an awesome destiny. God blessed Israel with a heavenly call to global privilege, leadership, and service. Such a calling requires extraordinary humility and loyalty. *So God brought them through a desert.* He was testing them to see if they were worthy of their calling. He was preparing them for a unique and incredible promotion – a place in history beyond compare. So it's easy to see why God had to test them. He had to know He could trust them with such an important assignment. He had to prepare them to be His noble ambassador to the nations.

"Remember how the LORD your God led you all the way in the wilderness these forty years, to humble and test you in order to know what was in your heart, whether or not you would keep his commands. He humbled you, causing you to hunger and then feeding you with manna, which neither you nor your ancestors had known, to teach you that man does not live on bread alone but on every word that comes from the mouth of the LORD. Your clothes did not wear out and your feet did not swell during these forty years. Know then in your heart that as a man disciplines his son, so the LORD your God disciplines you" (Deut. 8:2-5 NIV).

Read that last line again. The Lord's discipline is not merely corrective. It is preparatory. It is a loving Father training His children for a royal birthright in the Kingdom! "It is for discipline that you have to endure. God is treating you as sons. For what son is there whom his father does not discipline? ... He disciplines us for our good, that we may share his holiness. For the moment all discipline seems painful rather than pleasant, but later it yields the peaceful fruit of righteousness to those who have been trained by it" (Heb. 12:7,10-11 ESV).

The Lord wanted future generations to understand that the wilderness was not originally intended to be discipline for sin. Nor was it a mistake, or God's inability to keep His promises. *Israel's desert was a training ground for greatness.* It was their "wilderness of promotion."

29

It is the same for us. God has given each believer the highest calling conceivable – to "share His holiness" (Heb. 12:10 NASB). What does it mean to share His holiness? Listen to the way Paul puts it. "And we know that for those who love God all things work together for good, for those who are called according to his purpose. For those whom he foreknew he also predestined to be conformed to the image of his Son, in order that he might be the firstborn among many brothers" (Rom. 8:28-29 ESV).

Each of us is called to be like Jesus. That's what it means to share His holiness. We are called to share *His nature* – to personify our Lord in love, character, wisdom, and power. This is why God saved us. He justified us so He could mold us into the image of His precious Son. Then the world could see the glory of God – live and in person – through us. Is there any higher calling? Is there any more grand and noble purpose? What a privilege to be called into God's family. And just as our general call is to unveil Christ to the world, our specific call is to unveil Him within our *particular* spheres of influence – our relationships, vocations, neighborhoods, and gifts.

30

This means we need training. We must learn how to rely on God and not ourselves. We have to allow God to turn us into beautiful, whole vessels of the Holy Spirit that no longer live out of our fleshly desires, but out of Christ's character. How priceless is His image in us! Just as our souls could not be purchased with gold and silver, but only with precious blood, so Christ's image cannot be cultivated cheaply. Yes, it is a gift given freely when we believe. But its "working out" in daily life is costly (Phil. 2:12). We cannot become seasoned saints, expressing Christ naturally in the most pressing of circumstances, overnight. Such maturity doesn't happen in a microwave. We need more than a class or a church meeting. We can't even catch it at a revival service. (Though all of these settings are necessary and provide us with valuable spiritual treasures.) No, becoming like Jesus only occurs in the rough and tumble of real life.

That is the purpose for the wilderness. When God wants to promote us to a new level of spiritual authority, He doesn't just whisk us into position. He prepares us. He trains and refines us before He can lift us into a new dimension of our destiny. If we resist the process, we resist the promotion. It's that simple.

The wilderness is the process. It is a dry, difficult time when God strips us of self-support and compels us to look to Him in a new way. God does not want superficial people. He does not want children who know how to act spiritual in church or when life is easy, but when serious pressure or injustice comes, react just as the world would. God wants a people like His Son – fully developed, spiritual people who have gone through raw wastelands and emerged shining like stars. "When He has tested me, I shall come forth as gold" (Job 23:10).

God's hammer and chisel forge into such people real character, faith, and maturity. They've had a genuine, ground level experience with God. Now they look like Jesus: meek, loving, powerful, and real. You can't get such results quickly. You can't get them cheaply. They come only through God's painful cauldron, and result in the sweet spirit of Christ's character.

Israel's path to the Promised Land went through the wilderness. Because they resisted through complaints and rebellion, the first generation wandered in the wilderness till they died without destiny. Likewise, before Joseph fulfilled his dream of greatness, he was molded in the dry outback of rejection, pit, and prison. Through it all he remained loyal to God and became the most powerful man in the world next to Pharaoh. But he had to be prepared for such glory. The teenager who boasted of his dreams may have been a good boy, but he was hardly ready for ruling Egypt. He needed years of serious heat to become God's man. Even Jesus, "although he was a son, he learned obedience through what he suffered. And being made perfect, he became the source of eternal salvation to all who obey him" (Heb. 5:8-9 ESV). Before promotion there must be process; before resurrection there must be death.

We cannot bypass the Lord's discipline. Some have tried and brought compromise or ruin to their lives. They sought to bypass the wilderness because "they did not know My ways" (Heb. 3:10 NASB). They wanted the prize without the price, the success without the school, the crown without the cross. But God doesn't work that way. The path to glory passes through barren lands. So assess your situation. Consider if you are in a wilderness of promotion.

Perhaps the Spirit is using this booklet to confirm your spiritual location in the wilderness of promotion. If so, you have a wonderful advantage. You can accurately assess your situation, know what God is doing, and know how to respond. Repent if you've fought God and complained. Turn to the Lord and listen to His Spirit. Take heart. God is with you. Believe His promises no matter how they contradict your circumstances. Confess them with real faith before it gets too easy to matter. Insist on obeying and trusting Him. Let the process mold you into Christ's image. You will have great reward and fulfill your destiny. As Smith Wigglesworth said, "Only melted gold is minted."

When God wants to drill a man,

And thrill a man,

And skill a man

When God wants to mold a man

To play the noblest part;

When He yearns with all His heart

To create so great and bold a man

That all the world shall be amazed,

Watch His methods, watch His ways!
How He ruthlessly perfects
Whom He royally elects!
How He hammers him and hurts him,
And with mighty blows converts him
Into trial shapes of clay which
Only God understands;
While his tortured heart is crying
And he lifts beseeching hands!
How He bends but never breaks
When his good He undertakes;
How He uses whom He chooses,
And which every purpose fuses him;
By every act induces him
To try His splendor out—
God knows what He's about.

~ Author Unknown

Survival Tip #3

Find Shelter

Someone stranded in a physical survival situation must immediately find or build a shelter. The first great danger is exposure to the desert's harsh elements. It's crucial to maintain your core body temperature in order to endure. Direct sunlight and extreme heat cause heatstroke. Rain and cold cause hypothermia. A good shelter provides the necessary shade or warmth to keep your body temperature as stable as possible.

This expert advice mirrors spiritual life well. Listen to one of God's promises, borrowing language from Israel's wilderness journey: "Over everything the glory will be a canopy. It will be a shelter and shade from the heat of the day, and a refuge and hiding place from the storm and rain" (Isa. 4:5-6 NIV). Those finding themselves in a spiritual desert must embrace this promise, immediately seeking God as the wilderness shelter that will protect them from harsh elements.

We may be tempted to equate "desert" with God's absence. But nothing could be further from the truth. Barren lands lack many conveniences, but they never lack God's presence! A child of God is never cut off from Him. On the contrary, God's presence is our safe place in the desert *more than ever*. Remember, one of our key resources in the wilderness is the comfort of the Holy Spirit. God is always with us, but in the howling void of the wilderness, we can actually come to know His presence in new and greater dimensions.

This truth is an answer to Moses' wilderness prayer centuries ago. "If Your presence does not go with us, do not send us up from here" (Exod. 33:15 NASB). God assured him, "My presence shall go with you, and I will give you rest" (Exod. 33:14). The one thing Israel did in fact have was the precious companionship of their unique, powerful, and loving God. They were not alone in the wilderness. God was with them, and God is with you – *earnestly* with you.

So the way a child of God finds or builds a shelter is by seeking God all the more diligently as a haven in the desert, and by *establishing* the habit of running to and remaining in Him. Use the spiritual desert as an excuse to discover God afresh as your "refuge and strength." Practice taking sanctuary in His presence throughout your day through prayer and worship. It will protect you from the unforgiving, unrelenting elements of spiritual deserts.

Demonic forces wander about in these arid conditions, the "waterless places" of life (Matt. 12:43 NASB). They try to take advantage of those spending time in God's testing grounds. But even in such intensified circumstances, you can remain hidden in Christ, shielded and safe within an impenetrable fortress made of walls a thousand miles thick. It is a still, enclosed garden amid the chaos outside. It will keep your spiritual "core body temperature" stable as if you were not really under such extreme conditions. "They will neither hunger nor thirst, nor will the desert heat or the sun beat down on them" (Isa. 49:10 NIV). How can this be? How can our most vulnerable time be our most protected and durable time? Because *God* "is our refuge and strength, a very present help in trouble" (Psa. 46:1).

"Whoever dwells in the shelter of the Most High will rest in the shadow of the Almighty. I will say of the Lord, 'He is my refuge and my fortress, my God, in whom I trust.' Surely he will save you from the fowler's snare and from the deadly pestilence. He will cover you with his feathers, and under his wings you will find refuge; his faithfulness will be your shield and rampart. You will not fear the terror of night, nor the arrow that flies by day, nor the pestilence that stalks in the darkness, nor the plague that destroys at midday. A thousand may fall at your side, ten thousand at your right hand, but it will not come near you. You will only observe with your eyes and see the punishment of the wicked. If you say, 'The Lord is my refuge,' and you make the Most High your dwelling, no harm will overtake you, no disaster will come near your tent" (Psa. 91:1-10 NIV).

Think about this. When did God first promise He would abide with His people? When did He establish His presence with them? When did He give specific instructions for building His tabernacle in the middle of their camp? In the wilderness! That was the very time He inaugurated His personal, permanent presence with Israel. To this day Jews celebrate the "Feast of Booths," a festival celebrating the season when they lived in tents in the wilderness, and God lived in a tent among them. The wilderness is not the place of God's absence. It is the place where He establishes His presence in a fresh way.

Never is God more "with" His people than in the wilderness. Never is God more present to you than while you traverse spiritual deserts. People often testify that, during the most difficult times in their lives, God's presence becomes more pronounced to their souls than usual. You will often hear them say things like, "I wouldn't trade that experience for the world." In the midst of pain and suffering they come to know the presence of Jesus more intimately and experience Him more powerfully.

You can experience Him this way also. But you must make Him your shelter in the desert. No matter how discouraged you feel, rouse yourself to seek Him. Wrap yourself in His love and truth. Take time to conceal yourself in Him by spending time in His presence. *Make His faithfulness your shield and shelter* (Psa. 91:4). Know that you are hidden away deeply in a divine fortress that the harsh, demonic elements cannot penetrate. "Even though I walk through the valley of the shadow of death, I fear no evil, for You are with me … you prepare a table before me in the presence of my enemies … Surely goodness and mercy will follow me all the days of my life, *and I will dwell in the house of the Lord forever*" (Psa. 23:4-6 NASB).

41

Survival Tip #4

Build a Fire

Another priority for physical survival in the desert is building a fire. The fire's heat can dry wet clothes and keep the body warm in cold conditions. It can also purify water by boiling it. Experts say that fire even has the psychological effect of boosting morale during a survival situation. Its warmth and light give comfort and restore confidence. This helps the stranded person calm down and think more logically.

We need these advantages of fire for our spiritual lives also. Wilderness seasons make us vulnerable to negative attitudes. Sorrow can soak us like a cold rain. Anger can sneak in and contaminate the thoughts we think. And the desert's big danger, disillusionment, can blind us to the hope of the Lord's faithfulness that leads us out to the Promised Land. But God's fire consumes these dangers. It dries out sorrow, boils away the impurity of anger, and emits a glow in the desert night that restores faith. Divine fire brings revival in the wilderness.

But what does it look like practically? What is God's "fire" for a personal desert? The story of Israel's time in the wilderness again provides the answer.

As we saw, Israel's desert period was God's appointed time to establish His presence with His people. "So Moses finished the work. Then the cloud covered the tent of meeting, and the glory of the LORD filled the tabernacle" (Exod. 40:33-34). That's the moment when God took up residence among His people. But that was just the beginning. God was establishing even more for His people during their formative time in the wilderness.

44

Once He established His presence among them, God had to institute a way for His people to approach Him. In other words, *He had to teach them how to worship Him.* And what was at the center of the worship He gave them? Fire. "Moses and Aaron went into the tent of meeting. When they came out and blessed the people, the glory of the Lord appeared to all the people. *Then fire came out from before the Lord* and consumed the burnt offering and the portions of fat on the altar;

and when all the people saw it, they shouted and fell on their faces" (Lev. 9:23-24 NASB).

What, therefore, is our "fire" during a personal wilderness? *It is passionate, sacrificial worship.* Trials or dry spells are not the times to allow the flames of devotion to cool down. Those are the very times to burn the brightest. Wholehearted, sacrificial worship is what keeps our gaze fixed on the beauty and truth of Jesus Christ during difficult times. It keeps our hearts ablaze with love and adoration. *That* is the fire that keeps sorrow, anger, and disillusionment out of our hearts. What coldness or impurity can withstand the flames of divine love? What demonic predator dares come near a saint torching the night with an inferno of worship? Fiery devotion terrorizes our enemies and acts as a defense against desert dangers. Most of all, though, it pleases God.

45

It's important to remember, however, that Israel did not start its own fire. The Lord did. Those stranded in a physical wilderness without matches or a lighter must start their own fire with the raw materials nature provides them. That can be a challenge for those without experience in survival techniques. But this is one challenge that does not carry over to the spiritual wilderness. We never have to worry about lighting our own fire. Just as fire came out from the Lord's presence for Israel's altar, so does He ignite the flames in our hearts. Father God already gave us the Holy Spirit when we were born again. The Lord Jesus then baptizes us in the Holy Spirit by grace. The spirit of worship comes from God as a gift. We don't have to look to our surrounding circumstances for inspiration. We can look to the Lord and rediscover the great fire that burns within.

Yet it is our job to keep that fire burning. God starts it, but commands us to maintain it. "The fire must be kept burning on the altar continuously; it must not go out" (Lev. 6:13 NIV). We must partner with the Lord as stewards of worship in the desert. Paul tells us, "I appeal to you therefore, brothers, by the mercies of God, to *present your bodies as a living sacrifice*, holy and acceptable to God, which is your spiritual worship" (Rom. 12:1 ESV). Later he adds, "*Fervent in Spirit*, serving the Lord" (Rom. 12:11 NKJV). God gave us the Spirit, but we are responsible to stoke His flames by worshipping Him during hard times. Thus Paul exhorts believers to activate the Spirit's existing flame: "And do not get drunk with wine, for that is debauchery, but be filled with the Spirit, addressing one another in psalms and hymns and spiritual songs, singing and making melody to the Lord with your heart, giving thanks always and for everything to God the Father in the name of our Lord Jesus Christ" (Eph. 5:18-20 ESV).

Worship touches God's depths when it burns from our depths. The Lord did not wait to establish Israel's worship until they settled in Canaan. He set them on fire in the desert, *before* the Promised Land. He could not afford for them to learn to worship only after gaining public success and identity. He had to teach them to worship *in order* to forge their identity. Otherwise their worship would be "strange fire," a self-serving religious façade without presence or substance – without God Himself.

Israel's character had to be tempered by fire while suffering in Sinai's badlands. They couldn't light themselves on fire once they arrived. They had to emerge from the wilderness already ablaze with God. For this reason the Lord appeared privately to Moses in a burning desert bush. He was symbolizing His people's essential identity. *Israel was a bush in the desert flaming with God*. God took that bush as it burned with His glory, and planted it in the Promised Land.

47

It is the same for us. God brings us into the wilderness *to set us on fire*. Then He can bring people into their destiny who have learned to worship – truly *worship* – Him with loyal, fervent hearts. We cannot become pure sacrifices of love if we learn to worship only under the most ideal conditions, during exciting services, to the coolest music, and with the best musicians. We must learn to worship in the wilderness. If we won't burn for God in the desert, then we won't burn for Him at all. Conversely, if we will worship in the obscurity of the wilderness, then God can use us in public. For then our flames consist of white-hot glory, rather than carnal passion. This is how God creates true worshippers. So don't waste your wilderness. Make it a temple of glory.

If you've lost the sense of His fire amid the harsh conditions of your personal desert, then turn to God again. You possess God's flame burning inside you. Fellowship with the Spirit within, and find again His zeal to glorify Jesus and adore the Father. Open your heart in spite of your circumstances and natural feelings, and allow adoration to flow out of your mouth. Remember His amazing grace, His steadfast love, and His gift of Jesus Christ to you. Give thanks with passion. Worship with affection. Not because you feel like it, but because the Lord is worthy – *especially* in the desert. When you put yourself on the altar like this, God's flames will consume you as a living sacrifice. And the resulting fire will protect your heart, nurture your soul, and illumine your night. Engulf your wilderness in a blaze of worship!

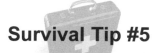

Survival Tip #5

Drink Water

Hydration is essential to survive a natural wilderness. It is also essential to survive a supernatural wilderness. Just as drinking clean water is urgent in hot, dry weather, we must drink in God's presence during desert seasons. "You, God, are my God, earnestly I seek you. I thirst for you, my whole being longs for you, in a dry and parched land where there is no water" (Psa. 63:1 NIV). Survival experts even warn us not to wait till we feel thirsty, but to drink as much as possible to keep the hydration level of our bodies high. Likewise, it is critical that those in a spiritual wilderness constantly be filled with God's Spirit. "Everyone who drinks this [natural] water will be thirsty again, but whoever drinks the water I give him will never thirst" (John 4:13-14 NIV).

God's provision for Israel in the wilderness applies to us today: "All drank the same spiritual drink, for they were drinking from a spiritual rock which followed them; and the rock was Christ" (1 Cor. 10:4 NASB). Our refreshment in the wilderness is God's presence, and God's presence is the Holy Spirit. Just as the Holy Spirit is our comfort, shelter, and fire, so also is He, like water, the essence of life for our whole being. Jesus said, "If anyone is thirsty, let him come to Me and drink. He who believes in Me, as the Scripture said, 'From his innermost being will flow rivers of living water'" (John 7:37-38 NASB).

Scripture often relates the Holy Spirit to water. Joel declares Israel's future restoration by reminding them that God "has poured down for you the rain, the early and latter rain as before" (Joel 2:23 NASB). He then transfers this image to the gift of the Spirit: "I will *pour out* my Spirit on all people" (Joel 2:28 NIV). When Joel's prophecy was fulfilled on the day of Pentecost, it says that the disciples were "all *filled* with the Holy Spirit" – as if with water – "and began to speak with other tongues, as the Spirit gave them utterance" (Acts 2:4).

If God's "liquid" presence is the Spirit, how then can we "drink" or "be filled with" His Spirit? How can we remain "hydrated" by the Spirit's presence while

52

crossing a dry spiritual landscape? We do this by *praying in the Spirit*. Listen to what Paul told Christians in the midst of intense battle: "Through every kind of prayer and petition, *pray at all times in the Spirit*" (Eph. 6:18 NASB). And Jude tells believers facing trouble, "You, beloved," keep yourselves in God's love by "building yourselves up on your most holy faith, *praying in the Holy Spirit*" (Jude 20-21).

How, then, do we pray in the Spirit? We pray in the Spirit when we connect with His presence, partner with His leading, and permit Him to empower our prayers. When we follow His leadership, He not only shows us the right things to pray, but also gives us the energy to pray them (Rom. 8:26-27). The important thing is to allow His expressions – His feelings and "language" – to mesh with our feelings and language. That is praying in the Spirit.

The Spirit expresses Himself through us in several ways. He praises and thanks God with many different kinds of songs (Eph. 5:18-19). Sometimes He makes groans too deep for words (Rom. 8:23). He may cry out with affection and childlike need for God as our "Abba" (Gal. 4:6), or declare Christ's awesome lordship over an impossible situation (1 Cor. 12:3). The Spirit's bank of prayer language contains deep adoration of God's majesty and Christ's sacrifice (Rev. 4-5), as well as pleas

53

for Jesus to return (Rev. 22:17). The Holy Spirit has a broad treasury of language for every kind of situation and emotion we may face. My point is this. Praying in the Spirit means getting close to Him, sensing His mood, hearing His voice, and cooperating with His specific expression in any given moment.

But there's one expression of the Spirit I want to spotlight, since it most effectively refreshes us in the desert. That expression is *praying in tongues*. The person speaking in an unknown tongue edifies himself (1 Cor. 14:4). Praying in tongues by the Spirit is an unobstructed connection to God's hydrating power in the wilderness. It enables us to pray in a way that's not restricted by our understanding or limited by our native language. "For one who speaks in a tongue speaks to not men but to God; for no one understands him, but he utters mysteries in the Spirit" (1 Cor. 14:2 ESV). Unknown tongues may not help a gathering of believers (since no one understands the one speaking), but it greatly helps the individual who needs potent spiritual rehydration.

This is because praying in tongues *edifies* the person praying. The verb, "edify," means more than "encourage." The original word actually means "to construct, strengthen, or restore." In other words, through speaking in tongues, the Spirit not only encourages our hearts, but also *builds* our inner person. He takes the blessings we inherited when we believed (Eph. 1:3), and progressively connects them to assemble us into powerful people. So praying in the Spirit, praying in other tongues, *fortifies* us. It constructs and strengthens us in the desert.

Consider how powerful it is when we pray in our native language. The Bible teaches that when we pray heavy burdens off our chest, God replaces them with supernatural peace (Phil. 4:6-7). Also, praising God amid our problems, when breakthrough comes, brings joy to our hearts. That joy then becomes our strength, even if the problems persist (Neh. 8:10). Now what if we were able to intercede or praise from places too deep for our conscious mind to access? What if we were able to pray prayers we *needed* to pray, but could never articulate in our native language?

This is what praying in tongues does for us. It enables us to pray straight from our spirit without the limits of our mind. "For if I pray in a tongue, *my spirit prays*, [though] my mind is unfruitful" (1 Cor. 14:14 NASB). Such praying is not only free of blockage and carnality, but it's also laser accurate. When God answers *these* prayers, or when we experience the rapture of *this* praise, we receive measures of peace, joy, and strength that can come no other way. These are the virtues that

55

fortify us from within, filling us with "streams in the desert" from the internal springs of the Spirit. They enable us to range the desert as healthy, creative people full of faith and spiritual vitality for others.

If you're in a spiritual desert, keep yourself hydrated. Drink deeply and often of your internal resources by praying in the Spirit. Allow Jesus to baptize you in the Holy Spirit, or rediscover the depths of such a wonderful immersion in His presence. By faith, open your mouth and allow the Spirit to give you utterances that your mind doesn't understand. Develop the habit in the desert that will *always* keep you saturated with God. It will quench your thirst, fortify your soul, and keep you from spiritual dehydration during dry times.

Survival Tip #6

Find Nourishment

Finding a source of food in the wilderness helps the survivor keep energy and focus. There are different kinds of plants that can be eaten in the wild, but some are poisonous. So a person must take great care in what he or she eats when stranded without provisions. That's why it is ideal to learn what is edible before an emergency situation. Unfortunately, not everyone gets this luxury.

As God's people, however, we do get that luxury. We already know our source of nourishment in the wilderness. It is always healthy, always pure. And as I mentioned under the second survival tip, it is always available. Israel refused it in their wilderness, but Jesus welcomed it in His: "Man shall not live by bread alone, but *by every word that comes from the mouth of God*" (Matt. 4:4).

This verse means that, along with the Spirit, God's *Word* is the essence of human life. True life is not defined by our natural existence or sustenance ("eating bread"). It's not even defined by arriving at our destined place in life, like a land flowing with milk and honey. True life is the eternal life that only comes through God's Word. "In the beginning was the Word, and the Word was with God, and the Word was God. He was in the beginning with God. All things came into being through Him, and apart from Him nothing came into being that has come into being. *In Him was life*, and the life was the Light of men" (John 1:1-4 NASB). Jesus Himself is this Word, and He said, "The *words* that I have spoken to you are spirit *and are life*" (John 6:63 NASB). That means the way we relate to God's words is the way we relate to Jesus, who is life itself. Thus He told religious people who opposed Him, "You search the Scriptures because you think that in them you have eternal life; it is these that testify about Me; and you are unwilling to come to Me *so that you may have life*" (John 5:39-40 NASB).

60   This truth is so important, that God specifically led His people into the wilderness to teach it to them. He led them into a difficult situation, humbled them, and allowed them to go hungry so they would discover in the deepest way possible that trusting and obeying

God's Word is life itself (Deut. 8:2-3). "Before I was afflicted I went astray, but now I keep your word" (Psa. 119:67). Therefore, God takes *us* through a spiritual wilderness so we will learn to keep His Word. The good Christian duty of "reading our Bibles" is not enough. Our Father's purpose is for us to *live* by His every Word. There are two aspects of this that deserve our attention.

First, "living" by the Word means feasting on its truth till it becomes our way of thinking. It's one thing to read our Bible; it's another thing to devour its words until, as one preacher put it, "they devour You." God's Word must become our mental culture, a way of thinking transformed from the natural to the divine (Rom. 12:2). This is why I talk about "feasting" on the Word. We cannot merely read our Bibles to log devotional time. We must share Jeremiah's appetite: "When I discovered your words, I devoured them. They are my joy and my heart's delight" (Jer. 15:16). And the Psalmist said, "How sweet are Your words to my taste! Yes, sweeter than honey to my mouth!" (Psa. 119:103 NASB).

61

This means we conform our old thought patterns to God's way of thinking as revealed in Scripture. We read, we study, we meditate, we confess, we declare, we memorize. We *bombard* ourselves with God's Word till it starts to reshape the creases in our brains and talk back to us. "My son, keep your father's commandment, and forsake not your mother's teaching. Bind them on your heart always; tie them around your neck. When you walk, they will lead you; when you lie down, they will watch over you; and when you awake, they will talk with you" (Prov. 6:20-22 ESV).

With the Word of God sculpted into our souls, our lives morph into its shape. Then we're not just reading the Word, but *living* by it. The wilderness is the very time designated by God for us to make His Word the ultimate source of our lives. The Word is, after all, the only thing we have to live on. But then again, it's the only thing we need. It is our feast in the wilderness.

Second, "living" by the Word means obeying the Word. Obedience to God is always important. But it's especially important in the wilderness, because that is the time when God is testing us to see if we will obey. If we won't obey during difficult times, we won't obey in easy times.

The author of Hebrews warned Christian friends going through a spiritual wilderness, "Today if you hear His voice, do not harden your hearts as when they provoked Me, as in the day of trial in the wilderness, where your fathers tried Me by testing Me, and saw My works for forty years. Therefore I was angry with this generation, and said, 'They always go astray in their heart, and they did not know My ways'; as I swore in My wrath, 'They shall not enter My rest'" (Heb. 3:7-11 NASB).

He went on to explain, "To whom did He swear that they would not enter His rest, but to those who were disobedient? So we see that they were not able to enter because of unbelief" (Heb. 3:18-19 NASB). Thus He used strong terms to warn His Church against disobedience in a spiritual wilderness. Just as God disciplined Israel, so would He discipline them if they continued to disobey. Suffering a difficult season was no excuse for violating God's Word.

Now let's look a little closer. The author of Hebrews linked obedience to faith like two sides of the same coin. The two words were interchangeable in the verse quoted just above. God banned Israel from the Promised Land for disobedience in the first sentence, and for unbelief in the second. Their lack of faith led to their disobedience. Their disobedience indicated their lack of faith. Further, the author made very clear exactly what "word" Israel disbelieved and disobeyed. "For indeed we have had good news preached to us, just as they also; but *the word they heard* did not profit them, because it was not united by faith in those who heard" (Heb. 4:2 NASB).

63

So Israel did not believe "the word they heard." Specifically, the "word" Israel rejected was *God's promise that they would enter the Land of their destiny!* God pledged them a land flowing with milk and honey. He promised them a good and spacious land where they would enjoy security and have rest from their enemies. Indeed, He would liberate them from bondage and personally escort them into the home of their dreams Himself. This was His promise, His "word" to them.

After centuries of slavery in Egypt, what exhilaration they must have felt when they "heard" this promise. What delight they must have taken in the dream-come-true "word" declaring their own country, identity, and freedom. Yet here they were in a desert – no milk, no honey, no safety, no inheritance, *no promise fulfilled*. Months earlier, as the Red Sea parted before their eyes, God's promises must have felt so real to them! They must have almost tasted their Land's fruit and smelled its lilies. But instead: dust, danger, rocks, thirst, serpents, and fears – the desert. God said, "Promised Land," but then He led them into the wilderness. Instead of entering their glory, they were wandering in a wasteland, battling cruel elements, and scrounging for strange food every morning.

Israel faced a predicament. The word of God that promised a glorious future now looked absurd in the barren wilderness of shattered dreams. The "word they heard," instead of inspiring hope through fulfillment, now seemed to hang suspended above them, just out of reach, sneering and jeering at them as they roamed the desert. Israel was caught in that long, strange tension between promise and fulfillment, between God's integrity and circumstances that appeared to contradict His Word. But that was the very time they needed to believe. If they would have *believed* God's Word amid such crisis, then they would have *obeyed* it and profited from it. Since they did not believe, they did not obey – and did not receive its benefits. God put them in this situation and watched to see what kind of people He had.

Their response was regrettable. They complained about their conditions. They longed for their days of slavery in Egypt. They worshipped idols. They committed immorality. They criticized their leadership. They tested the Lord who delivered them and promised them something good. And when they heard about the inhabitants of their "Promised Land," they said, "If only we had died in Egypt, or even here in the wilderness! Why is the Lord taking us to this country only to have us die in battle? Our wives and our little ones will be carried off as plunder! Wouldn't it be better for us to return to Egypt? Let's choose a new leader and go back to Egypt!" (Num. 14:2-4 NLT).

No wonder God was angry with them. They questioned His faithfulness based on what their natural senses perceived, rather than on what God said. Put another way, Israel wanted to live by bread alone and not every *word* that came from God's mouth. Their lack of faith turned into rebellion. They scorned God's promises and defied His directions. As a result, they did not benefit from the original "word they heard." They died in the wilderness without seeing the Promised Land.

Therefore, when we enter a spiritual wilderness, we must not confuse our situation with God's integrity. Living by His every word means *continuing to believe His promises even if they seem contradicted for the moment.* That's the whole point of the wilderness! When God declares to us, "Promised Land," He will usually take us through its opposite first – the desert. Those are the ways of God that Israel did not know. But they are the ways of God *we must know*.

In God's Kingdom, before the resurrection there must come death. Eternal life rises from a grave just as spring emerges from winter. The key is, we must understand these mysterious, divine ways and *believe* the word promising life during the season of death. Jesus declared this kind of faith on the cross when He said, "Father, into Your hands I commit My spirit" (Luke 23:46). So must we. God wants to see if we will believe His Word during the desert season, when He is stripping us of self-sufficiency before He fulfills that Word. If we do believe, that kind of faith gives us the strength to remain loyal to Him – to obey Him – in the wilderness. It keeps us from murmuring, criticizing, and worshipping false gods. And it prepares us for the reward of resurrection – entering the Promised Land.

Thus God's Word becomes our source of nourishment in the desert. For the desert itself will not offer spiritual sustenance to our weary souls. The devil will come during these seasons, point to the wilderness circumstances, and insist that God's promise is really a failure or that we misunderstood it. But we must resist his temptations. We must not feast on the situation as it stands, but continue to feast on God's Word by believing and obeying it – even when it seems absurd to do so. Remember: The reason God took us down the route of hard places is to see if we would still believe His Word *while there*. That's when it counts. The Word is our nourishment *in the desert*.

Hebrews offers one more thought about the Word for Christians in the desert. "For the word of God is living and active, sharper than any two-edged sword, piercing to the division of soul and of spirit, of joints and of marrow, and discerning the thoughts and intentions of the heart" (Heb. 4:12 ESV). At first this verse seems oddly placed in its context. The author had been discussing entering God's rest after a desert season. "Therefore let us be diligent to enter that rest, so that no one will fall, through following the same example of disobedience" (Heb. 4:11 NASB). Then suddenly in the next verse, he mentions that God's Word is sharper than a sword and able to dissect the deepest recesses of the human heart.

The "Word" of God's promise is a breath of inspiration when He first declares it in Egypt. But when that same Word – declaring "Promised Land!" – follows us into the desert, it becomes a sword that reveals the depths of our hearts. The *real* intentions of our hearts only become exposed when present circumstances flatly contradict the Word of promise. Only then is it clear if we *really* trusted God. Only then does that grey, blurry line between soul and spirit focus into a clear, dark line separating two ways of relating to God: on our terms (soul), or His (spirit). In other words, when God's Word of promise enters the wilderness with us, it accurately reveals whether we are truly loyal to God, or we merely wanted Him to serve our own interests.

It's easy to trust God's promises when all is well and we're in a good mood. But when life's music descends into minor keys, and dark clouds gather above, God's Word is more challenging to believe. That's when it's tempting to get frustrated and blame God – or at least friends or church leaders – for His Word's failure to perform. And those are the very moments it becomes clear if we are actually loyal to God *as God* – at all times, no matter what the circumstances – not just loyal to Him when it serves our selfish interests. Those who are proven to be people of "spirit" may not enjoy everything about the wilderness, but they are willing to embrace it. They know that only in the wilderness can God see if we are truly loyal to Him. Only in the wilderness does God's Word become a sword revealing our true spiritual grit.

If we know God's ways, we know that He brings life out of death. As we go through the desert of a kind of crucifixion, we must believe God's Word that promises life. So let's avoid Israel's example of disobedience. Don't resist God's Word when it seems contradicted by the wilderness. Feast on it! Devour it by replacing natural thinking with divine thinking, and by continuing to believe it when it opposes your circumstances. That is how to "live" by every word from God's mouth. That is how to be nourished in the desert.

69

Conclusion

The wilderness is an untamed place, a most difficult season for the human soul. But it can become the source of greatest spiritual reward. As we have seen in the history of Israel, as well as the life of Jesus Christ, God establishes His greatest works in the wilderness. In God's wisdom, life comes out of death, glory out of suffering, streams out of the desert. All of this happens so that God alone may be glorified for His marvelous handiwork in the lives of those who dare to be fashioned in barren places.

"I will open rivers on the bare heights, and fountains in the midst of the valleys. I will make the wilderness a pool of water, and the dry land springs of water. I will put in the wilderness the cedar, the acacia, the myrtle, and the olive. I will set in the desert the cypress, the plane and the pine together, that they may see and know, may consider and understand together, that the hand of the Lord has done this, the Holy One of Israel has created it" (Isa. 41:18-20 ESV).

But for this to happen we must remember God's purposes for the wilderness, and be determined to reap its benefits. The desert strips us of self-sufficiency, teaches us to rely totally on God, and molds us into the image of His Son. In other words, it increases God's glory in us by shaping us into human channels of divine life. "But we have this treasure in jars of clay, to show that the surpassing power belongs to God and not to us. We are afflicted in every way, but not crushed; perplexed, but not driven to despair; persecuted, but not forsaken; struck down, but not destroyed; always carrying in the body the death of Jesus, so that the life of Jesus may also be manifested in our bodies. For we who live are always being given over to death for Jesus' sake, *so that the life of Jesus also may be manifested in our mortal flesh*" (2 Cor. 4:7-11 ESV).

At the beginning of this booklet, I quoted Churchill who said, "If you're going through hell, keep going." For us this means, "If you're passing through a spiritual desert, don't waste it by grumbling or complaining; recognize God's purpose for it and don't quit till you make it through!" Yet the only way to do that is to put into action God's wisdom for the wilderness. That is what this spiritual survival guide was meant to help you do. So let's briefly summarize the six survival tips we covered:

1. <u>Don't panic</u> – Refuse natural fear and embrace God's love for you.

2. <u>Assess your situation</u> – Take stock of the resources God provided for your journey, and use them. Also, identify the kind of wilderness you're in so you will know how to navigate it.

3. <u>Find shelter</u> – Know that God is present to you now more than ever, and hide yourself in Him.

4. <u>Build a fire</u> – Set yourself ablaze with passionate worship for protection and purification.

5. <u>Drink water</u> – Keep yourself spiritually hydrated by praying at all times in the Spirit, especially with other tongues.

6. <u>Find nourishment</u> – Feast on God's Word through intense meditation, as well as radical faith and obedience.

When we adopt these words of wisdom for surviving hard times, we "clear the way for the Lord in the wilderness; make smooth in the desert a highway for our God" (Isa. 40:3 NASB). He is always with His children, but we pave a wider path for His involvement when we trust Him and walk in His ways. With the Lord at our side, even when things are hard, we can

73

emerge from the desert like Jesus, "in the power of the Spirit" (Luke 4:14). So take courage. Keep moving forward. The pain of the wilderness may be great, but greater still is its significance for your life. The Promised Land awaits you...

To find more resources by
Christ for all Nations & Daniel Kolenda
visit us online at

SHOP.CFAN.ORG

YOUR KINGDOM COME

The next great move of God will come as a result of **Prayer & Obedience** by the Body of Christ. Discover

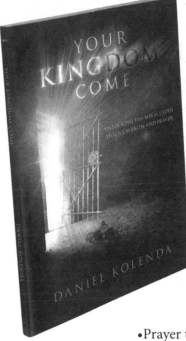

how God made us partners with Him for the fulfillment of His purposes in the earth. Don't miss your opportunity to purchase the **first book** released by Author and Evangelist Daniel Kolenda

IN THIS BOOK
LEARN ABOUT:

• Prayer that Delivers
• Prayer that Opens Doors
• Praying with Expectancy
•Prayer that Releases the Miraculous
• Prayer that Brings Heaven to Earth

Scan this QR Code with your Smart Phone for more information on this book. Or go to: *cfan.org/yourkingdomcome*

Healing in the GLORY

with Reinhard Bonnke
& Daniel Kolenda

This contemplative collection of songs is a comforting companion in times of prayer and meditation. If you need healing in your body, let the reading of the Word wash over you. It will comfort, uplift, and stir your faith to believe for your miracle.

FEATURES

- Scripture Read by Evangelists Reinhard Bonnke & Daniel Kolenda

- Music by World Class Pianist Steve Sensenig

- Classic Christian Music that is immediately recognizable

- 2 Disc Set includes an Instrumental Version for soaking or casual listening and a separate CD with Scripture and Music

SCAN THIS QR CODE
TO HEAR 1 SONG
& listen to samples
of all other tracks

A Great Outpouring
in Your Home Each Week

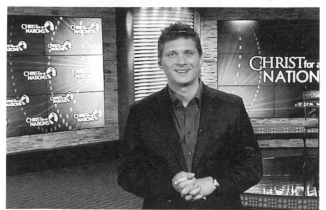

See **Daring Faith!**
Celebrate the **Miraculous!**
Find Your Answer!

Reinhard Bonnke and Daniel Kolenda invite you to experience
the powerful, life-changing ministry and miracles taking place as
we proclaim the Gospel and see new believers saved, healed and
delivered by the power of Jesus Christ.

Each week, you will meet ordinary people who've seen the extraordinary happen in their lives through the Lord's touch. Men,
women and children who were once broken, but now healed -
once in darkness, but now walking in the light of God's love.

*To see a complete television schedule or to
watch online visit us at CfaN.tv*

The Ministry of CHRIST FOR ALL NATIONS

Reinhard Bonnke
Evangelist &
Founder

Daniel Kolenda
Evangelist &
President

While he was just a young missionary in Lesotho, Reinhard Bonnke received a vision from God of "the continent of Africa being washed in the precious blood of Jesus." With this vision thundering in his soul, Reinhard Bonnke founded Christ for all Nations in 1974.

Since 1987, over 68 million people have made salvation decisions in the Gospel campaigns – completing a signed decision card. This harvest of souls could possibly be unparalleled in Church history.

Now, to ensure that this extraordinary harvest of souls will continue for as long as the opportunity lasts, Reinhard Bonnke has appointed a successor, Daniel Kolenda. Continuing in the same anointing for the same purpose, Daniel Kolenda has already seen over 10 million people come to Christ in the past four years. The ministry presses ever forward to see the completion of the vision – Africa is being saved!

For more information about the ministry of Evangelists Reinhard Bonnke & Daniel Kolenda please visit our website.

Offices in the USA • Germany • UK • Canada • South Africa
Singapore • Australia • Hong Kong • Nigeria